I0409716

Strategy for Homeland Defense and Civil Support

Department of Defense
Washington, D.C.

June 2005

Table of Contents

Foreword

Protecting the United States from direct attack is the highest priority of the Department of Defense. The military has traditionally secured the United States by projecting power overseas. While our current missions abroad continue to play a vital role for the security of our Nation, the terrorist attacks of September 11, 2001 emphasized that we are confronting fundamentally different challenges from those faced during the Cold War.

President George W. Bush activated all instruments of American power to respond to the attacks of September 11th, and directed the United States Government to better prepare for the reality of the 21st century threat. Working with Congress, President Bush established the Department of Homeland Security to prevent terrorist attacks in the United States. The Department of Defense, the traditional vanguard of America's security, began transforming as well. The stand-up of US Northern Command was an important first step—created to deter, prevent, and defeat aggression aimed at the United States.

The *Strategy for Homeland Defense and Civil Support* marks the next significant milestone in reshaping the Department's approach to homeland defense. Building upon the concept of an active, layered defense outlined in the *National Defense Strategy*, the *Strategy for Homeland Defense and Civil Support* constitutes the Department's vision for transforming homeland defense and civil support capabilities. It will fundamentally change the Department's approach to homeland defense in an historic and important way.

In the hands of the dedicated men and women of our military and the civilians who support them, I am confident the *Strategy for Homeland Defense and Civil Support* will improve significantly the Department's ability to counter the threats of the 21st century.

Gordon England
Deputy Secretary of Defense

Executive Summary

"The world changed on September 11, 2001. We learned that a threat that gathers on the other side of the earth can strike our own cities and kill our own citizens. It's an important lesson, one we can never forget. Oceans no longer protect America from the dangers of this world. We're protected by daily vigilance at home. And we will be protected by resolute and decisive action against threats abroad."

President George W. Bush
September 17, 2002

Protecting the United States homeland from attack is the highest priority of the Department of Defense (DoD). On September 11, 2001, the world changed dramatically. For the first time since Pearl Harbor, we experienced catastrophic, direct attacks against our territory. This time, however, the foe was not another nation but terrorists seeking to undermine America's political will and destroy our way of life. As a result, the United States has become a nation at war, a war whose length and scope may be unprecedented.

We now confront an enemy who will attempt to engage us not only far from US shores, but also at home. Terrorists will seek to employ asymmetric means to penetrate our defenses and exploit the openness of our society to their advantage. By attacking our citizens, our economic institutions, our physical infrastructure, and our social fabric, they seek to destroy American democracy. We dare not underestimate the devastation that terrorists seek to bring to Americans at home.

To defeat 21st century threats, we must think and act innovatively. Our adversaries consider US territory an integral part of a global theater of combat. We must therefore have a strategy that applies to the domestic context the key principles that are driving the transformation of US power projection and joint expeditionary warfare.

Secure the United States from Attack through an Active, Layered Defense

Directed by the Strategic Planning Guidance (March 2004), this Strategy for Homeland Defense and Civil Support focuses on achieving the Defense Department's paramount goal: securing the United States from direct attack. The Strategy is rooted in the following:

- Respect for America's constitutional principles;

- Adherence to Presidential and Secretary of Defense guidance;

- Recognition of terrorist and state-based threats to the United States; and

- Commitment to continue transformation of US military capabilities.

Protecting the United States in the ten-year timeframe covered by this Strategy requires an active, layered defense. **This active, layered defense is global, seamlessly integrating US capabilities in the forward regions of the world, the global commons of space and cyberspace, in the geographic**

approaches to US territory, and within the United States. It is a defense in depth. To be effective, it requires superior intelligence collection, fusion, and analysis, calculated deterrence of enemies, a layered system of mutually supporting defensive measures that are neither passive nor ad hoc, and the capability to mass and focus sufficient warfighting assets to defeat any attack.

This active, layered defense employs tactical defenses in a strategic offense. It maximizes threat awareness and seizes the initiative from those who would harm us. In so doing, it intends to defeat potential challengers before they threaten the United States at home.

Organizing Construct—Lead, Support, and Enable

Although the active, layered defense extends across the globe, this Strategy for Homeland Defense and Civil Support focuses primarily on DoD's activities in the US homeland and the approaches to US territory. In those geographic layers, the Department undertakes a range of activities to secure the United States from direct attack. These generally divide into the following categories:

- *Lead:* At the direction of the President or the Secretary of Defense, the Department of Defense executes military missions that dissuade, deter, and defeat attacks upon the United States, our population, and our defense critical infrastructure.

- *Support:* At the direction of the President or the Secretary of Defense, the Department of Defense provides support to civil authorities. This support is part of a comprehensive national response to prevent and protect against terrorist

incidents or recover from an attack or disaster. DoD provides support to a lead Federal agency when directed by the President or the Secretary of Defense.

- *Enable:* The Department of Defense seeks to improve the homeland defense and homeland security contributions of our domestic and international partners and, in turn, to improve DoD capabilities by sharing expertise and technology, as appropriate, across military and civilian boundaries.

Key Objectives of the Strategy

Within the lead, support, and enable framework for homeland defense and civil support, the Department is focused on the following paramount objectives, listed in order of priority:

- **Achieve maximum awareness of potential threats.** Together with the Intelligence Community and civil authorities, DoD works to obtain and promptly exploit all actionable information needed to protect the United States. Timely and actionable intelligence, together with early warning, is the most critical enabler to protecting the United States at a safe distance.

- **Deter, intercept and defeat threats at a safe distance.** The Department of Defense will actively work to deter adversaries from attacking the US homeland. Through our deterrent posture and capabilities, we will convince adversaries that threats to the US homeland risk unacceptable counteraction by the United States. Should deterrence fail, we will seek to intercept and defeat threats at a safe distance from the United States. When directed by the President or the Secretary of Defense, we will also defeat direct threats within US airspace and on US territory. In all cases, the Department of Defense cooperates closely with its domestic and international partners and acts in accordance with applicable laws.

- **Achieve mission assurance.** The Department of Defense performs assigned duties even under attack or after disruption. We achieve mission assurance through force protection, ensuring the security of defense critical infrastructure, and executing defense crisis management and continuity of operations (COOP).

- **Support civil authorities in minimizing the damage and recovering from domestic chemical, biological, radiological, nuclear, or high-yield explosive (CBRNE) mass casualty attacks.** The Department of Defense will be prepared to provide forces and capabilities in support of domestic CBRNE consequence management, with an emphasis on preparing for multiple, simultaneous mass casualty incidents. DoD's responses will be planned, practiced, and carefully integrated into the national response.

With the exception of a dedicated command and control element (currently the Joint Task Force-Civil Support) and the Army National Guard Weapons of Mass Destruction (WMD) Civil Support Teams, DoD will rely on dual-capable forces for the domestic consequence management mission. These dual-capable forces must be trained, equipped, and ready to provide timely assistance to civil authorities in times of domestic CBRNE catastrophes, programming for this capability when directed.

- **Improve national and international capabilities for homeland defense and homeland security.** The Department of Defense is learning from the experiences of domestic and international partners and sharing expertise with Federal, state, local, and tribal authorities, the private sector, and US allies and friends abroad. By sharing expertise, we improve the ability of the Department of Defense to carry out an active, layered defense.

Capabilities for Homeland Defense and Civil Support

Consistent with the National Defense Strategy's call to develop and sustain key operational capabilities, the Strategy for Homeland Defense and Civil Support promotes the development of core capabilities to achieve its objectives. Prominent capability themes include:

- **Intelligence, Surveillance, and Reconnaissance Capabilities.** The Department of Defense requires current and actionable intelligence identifying potential threats to US territory. DoD must also ensure that it can identify and track suspect traffic approaching the United States. DoD must conduct reconnaissance and surveillance to examine wide areas of the maritime and air domains and, working with lead domestic partners and Canada and Mexico in the land domain, discover potential threats before they reach the United States.

- **Information-Sharing.** Together with domestic and international partners, DoD will integrate and share information collected from a wide range of sources. The events of September 11, 2001 highlighted the need to share information across Federal agencies and, increasingly, with state, local, and tribal authorities, the private sector, and international partners.

- **Joint Operational Capabilities for Homeland Defense.** DoD will continue to transform US military forces to execute homeland defense missions in the forward regions, approaches, US homeland, and global commons.

- **Interagency and Intergovernmental Coordination.** The Department of Defense and our domestic and international partners will continue to cooperate closely in the execution of homeland defense and civil support missions.

When fully realized, this Strategy for Homeland Defense and Civil Support will transform and improve DoD capabilities in each of these areas.

Projected Implications of the Strategy

In developing this Strategy, the Department took into account its likely force structure, resource, and technology implications. Given scarce resources, this Strategy's objectives must be balanced against other priorities outlined in the National Defense Strategy. As DoD components implement the strategic tenets outlined in this document, a more

precise accounting of the forces, technological advances, and financial resources it requires will be needed.

Because DoD's forces and resources are finite, the Strategy recognizes the need to manage risks in the homeland defense and civil support mission areas. It therefore prioritizes DoD's efforts, focusing on the requirement to fulfill DoD's lead responsibilities for homeland defense. As a second priority, we will ensure the Department's ability to support civil authorities in recovering from multiple, catastrophic mass casualty CBRNE incidents within the United States.

The Department of Defense will expeditiously implement the Strategy for Homeland Defense and Civil Support. Fundamentally, this will require the Department to integrate strategy, planning, and operational capabilities for homeland defense and civil support more fully into DoD processes. **The Strategy for Homeland Defense and Civil Support is not a static document.** Even as the Department of Defense implements this Strategy, it will continue to adapt to changes in the strategic environment, incorporate lessons learned from operational experience, and capitalize on emerging technology and operational concepts.

4

I. Context

"For most of the twentieth century, the world was divided by a great struggle over ideas: destructive totalitarian visions or freedom and equality. That great struggle is over. The militant visions of class, nation, and race which promised utopia have been defeated and discredited. America is now threatened less by conquering states than we are by failing ones. We are menaced less by fleets and armies than by catastrophic technologies in the hands of the embittered few. We must defeat these threats to our Nation, allies, and friends."

The National Security Strategy of the United States of America

September 2002

The Strategy for Homeland Defense and Civil Support embodies the core principles articulated in the US Constitution, the Nation's laws, and in Presidential and Secretary of Defense guidance. It also responds to the challenges posed by the security environment over the next decade.

Key Definitions

Homeland security, as defined in the National Strategy for Homeland Security, is "a concerted national effort to prevent terrorist attacks within the United States, reduce America's vulnerability to terrorism, and minimize the damage and recover from attacks that do occur." The Department of Homeland Security is the lead Federal agency for homeland security. In addition, its responsibilities extend beyond terrorism to preventing, preparing for, responding to, and recovering from a wide range of major domestic disasters and other emergencies.

It is the primary mission of the Department of Homeland Security to prevent terrorist attacks within the United States. The Attorney General leads our Nation's law enforcement effort to detect, prevent, and investigate terrorist activity within the United States. Accordingly, the Department of Defense does not have the assigned responsibility to stop terrorists from coming across our borders, to stop terrorists from coming through US ports, or to stop terrorists from hijacking aircraft inside or outside the United States (these responsibilities belong to the Department of Homeland Security). Nor does DoD have the authority to seek out and arrest terrorists in the United States (these responsibilities belong to the Department of Justice).

Homeland defense is the protection of US sovereignty, territory, domestic population, and critical defense infrastructure against external threats and aggression, or other threats as directed by the President.[1] The Department of Defense is responsible for homeland defense.

Defense support of civil authorities, often referred to as civil support, is DoD support, including Federal military forces, the Department's career civilian and contractor personnel, and DoD agency and component

---

[1] Homeland Defense includes missions such as domestic air defense. The Department recognizes that threats planned or inspired by "external" actors may materialize internally. The reference to "external threats" does not limit where or how attacks could be planned and executed. The Department is prepared to conduct homeland defense missions whenever the President, exercising his constitutional authority as Commander in Chief, authorizes military actions.

assets, for domestic emergencies and for designated law enforcement and other activities. The Department of Defense provides defense support of civil authorities when directed to do so by the President or Secretary of Defense.

Standing Guidance from National and Defense Strategies

Directed by the Strategic Planning Guidance (March 2004), the Strategy for Homeland Defense and Civil Support integrates the objectives and guidance expressed in the National Security Strategy, the National Strategy for Homeland Security, and the National Defense Strategy to guide Department of Defense operations to protect the US homeland.

- The National Security Strategy (2002) expands the scope of US foreign and security policy to encompass forward-reaching preventive activities, including preemption, against hostile states and terrorist groups.

- The National Strategy for Homeland Security (2002) guides the national effort to secure the US homeland against terrorist attacks. It provides a framework for action at all levels of government that play a role in homeland security.

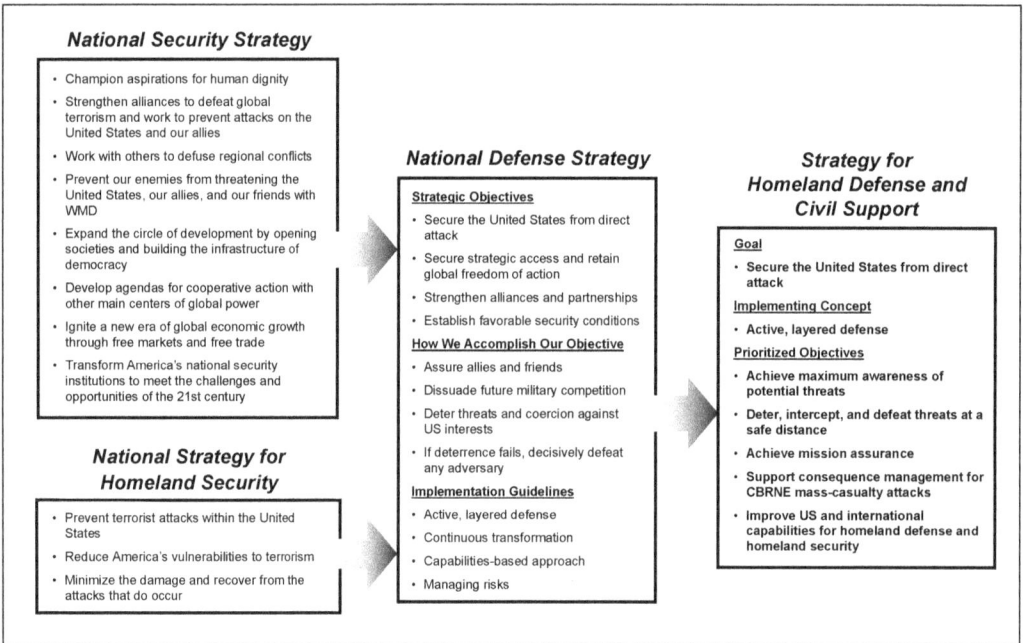

Figure 1: Strategic Underpinnings of the Homeland Defense and Civil Support Strategy

- The National Defense Strategy (2005) identifies as its top priority the dissuasion, deterrence, and defeat of direct threats to the United States. The Strategy's implementation hinges on an active, layered defense that is designed to defeat the most dangerous challenges early and at a safe distance, before they are allowed to mature. It directs military leadership to properly shape, size, and globally posture to 1) defend the US homeland; 2) operate in and from the forward regions;

3) swiftly defeat adversaries and achieve decisive, enduring results; and 4) conduct a limited number of lesser contingencies.

In addition to these overarching strategies, the Strategy for Homeland Defense and Civil Support is informed by, and complements, other key strategic and planning documents. These include standing National Security and Homeland Security Presidential Directives, the National Military Strategy, the National Military Strategic Plan for the War on Terrorism, the DoD Homeland Security Joint Operating Concept, and Military Transformation: A Strategic Approach (Office of the Director for Force Transformation).

Security Environment

The defining characteristic of the security environment over the next ten years is the risk of substantial, diverse, and asymmetric challenges to the United States, our allies, and interests. In this context, we are faced with great *uncertainty* regarding the specific character, timing, and sources of potential attacks. The Strategy for Homeland Defense and Civil Support aims to mitigate that uncertainty, addressing the full range of challenges to the US homeland over the next decade.

Nation-state military threats to the United States will persist throughout the next decade. Rogue nations, for example, pose immediate and continuing challenges to the United States and our allies, friends, and interests. In addition, we must prepare for the potential emergence of regional peer competitors.

The United States will also face a range of asymmetric, transnational threats. Of greatest concern is the availability of weapons of mass destruction, heretofore the exclusive domain of nation-states, to terrorist groups. **In the next ten years, these terrorist groups, poised to attack the United States and actively seeking to inflict mass casualties or disrupt US military operations, represent the most immediate challenge to the nation's security.**

Transnational terrorist groups view the world as an integrated, global battlespace in which to exploit perceived US vulnerabilities, wherever they may be. This battlespace includes the US homeland. Terrorists seek to attack the United States and its centers of gravity at home and abroad and will use asymmetric means to achieve their ends, such as simultaneous, mass casualty attacks. On September 11, 2001, terrorists demonstrated both the intent and capability to conduct complex, geographically dispersed attacks against the United States and our allies. It is foreseeable that adversaries will also develop or otherwise obtain chemical, biological, radiological, nuclear, or high-yield explosives (CBRNE) capabilities, with the intent of causing mass panic or catastrophic loss of life. Although America's allies and interests abroad will be the most likely targets of terrorism in the coming decade, we must also anticipate enemy attacks aimed at Americans at home.

Organizing for Homeland Defense and Civil Support

In light of the importance of homeland defense and DoD's contributions to homeland security, the Secretary of Defense, with the support of Congress, has improved the Department's organization and oversight structure for homeland defense and civil support.

- **The Assistant Secretary of Defense for Homeland Defense.** As stated in the 2003 National Defense Authorization Act, the

Assistant Secretary of Defense for Homeland Defense provides overall supervision of DoD's homeland defense activities. The establishment of the Assistant Secretary of Defense for Homeland Defense responded to the need for improved policy guidance to DoD Components on homeland defense and civil support issues.

- **Chairman of the Joint Chiefs of Staff.** The Chairman of the Joint Chiefs of Staff coordinates with and assists US Northern Command, US Pacific Command, the North American Aerospace Defense Command, and all other combatant commands with the strategic direction and planning for, as well as the execution of, homeland defense and civil support missions.

- **US Northern Command**, headquartered in Colorado Springs, Colorado. Established in 2002, US Northern Command (USNORTHCOM) is responsible for planning, organizing, and executing homeland defense and civil support missions within the continental United States, Alaska, and territorial waters. It also coordinates security cooperation with Canada and Mexico. In addition to the landmasses of the United States, Canada, and Mexico, US Northern Command's area of responsibility includes the coastal approaches, the Gulf of Mexico, Puerto Rico, and the US Virgin Islands.

- **US Pacific Command**, headquartered in Honolulu, Hawaii. US Pacific Command (USPACOM) has homeland defense and civil support responsibilities for Hawaii and US territories, possessions, and freely associated states in the Pacific.[2]

- **North American Aerospace Defense Command**, headquartered in Colorado Springs, Colorado. The bi-national North American Aerospace Defense Command (NORAD) is responsible for protecting the North American airspace over the United States and Canada. Aerospace warning and control are the cornerstones of the NORAD mission.

In addition to these organizations, all other regional and functional combatant commands, the Military Departments, and DoD elements contribute to the protection of the US homeland from attack.

- Other regional combatant commanders can promote international cooperation on homeland defense through exercises and military-to-military contact programs. Together with the functional combatant commanders, these regional commanders can also intercept and defeat adversaries intent on attacking US territory.

  Of particular note, US Strategic Command provides significant support to USNORTHCOM, USPACOM, and NORAD. US Strategic Command is responsible for planning, integrating, and coordinating global missile defense operations and support for missile defense, including providing warning of missile attack, across all combatant

---

[2] The Pacific territories, possessions, and freely associated states that are included in the US homeland are: Guam, American Samoa, and Jarvis Island; the Commonwealth of Northern Mariana Islands; the Freely Associated States under the Compacts of Free Association, which include the Federated States of Micronesia, the Republic of the Marshall Islands, and the Republic of Palau; and the following US possessions: Wake Island, Midway Islands, Johnston Island, Baker Island, Howland Island, Palmyra Atoll, Jarvis Island, and Kingman Reef.

commands. US Strategic Command is further charged with the global missions to undertake military space operations, to conduct information operations as well as computer network operations, and to integrate and synchronize DoD efforts in combating weapons of mass destruction.

- The Military Departments organize, train, and equip US military forces across operational domains. The Military Departments provide the bulk of the DoD capabilities likely to be requested for civil support.

- Other DoD Components contribute to homeland defense through intelligence collection, analysis, and prioritization; capability assessments; and oversight of relevant policy, acquisition, logistics, personnel, readiness, and financial matters.

The Strategy for Homeland Defense and Civil Support will guide all DoD Components across the full range of homeland defense and civil support activities.

Assumptions

This Strategy makes the following key assumptions:

- The United States will continue to face traditional military challenges emanating from hostile nation-states. Nation-state adversaries will incorporate asymmetric threats into their broader strategies of competition and confrontation with the United States.

- Terrorists will seek and potentially gain surreptitious entry into the United States to conduct mass casualty attacks against Americans on US soil.

  o Terrorists will exploit our vulnerabilities to create new methods of attack.

  o Terrorists and/or rogue states will attempt multiple, simultaneous mass casualty CBRNE attacks against the US homeland.

  o Terrorists will try to shape and degrade American political will in order to diminish American resistance to terrorist ideologies and agendas.

- Allies and friends will cooperate with the United States in mutually beneficial security cooperation arrangements.

- The Department of Homeland Security and other Federal, state, local, and tribal authorities will continue to improve their prevention, preparedness, response, and recovery capabilities throughout the decade.

- In the event of major catastrophes, the President will direct DoD to provide substantial support to civil authorities. DoD's responses will be planned, practiced, and carefully integrated into the national response.

- The likelihood of US military operations overseas will be high throughout the next ten years.

II. Active, Layered Defense

"The war on terror will not be won on the defensive. We must take the battle to the enemy, disrupt his plans, and confront the worst threats before they emerge. In the world we have entered, the only path to safety is the path of action. And this nation will act."

President George W. Bush
June 1, 2002

As set forth in the National Defense Strategy (2005), the Department of Defense is transforming its approach to homeland defense just as it is transforming national defense capabilities overall. **Guiding homeland defense planning is the concept of an active, layered defense, predicated on seizing the initiative from adversaries.**

"Our most important contribution to the security of the US homeland is our capacity to disrupt and defeat threats early and at a safe distance, as far from the US and its partners as possible. Our ability to identify and defeat threats abroad — before they can strike — while making critical contributions to the direct defense of our territory and population is the sine qua non of our nation's security."

The National Defense Strategy

The United States has multiple points of vulnerability that adversaries seek to exploit. Commerce relies on the flow of goods and people across the nation's borders, through our seaports and airports, and on our streets and highways. The US free market economy requires trust in the uninterrupted electronic movement of financial data and funds through cyberspace. The symbols of American heritage — monuments and public buildings — are a source of national pride and are open to all. Vast and potentially

vulnerable natural resources provide power to our homes and food for our tables.

To safeguard the American way of life and to secure our freedom we cannot depend on passive or reactive defenses. A strictly defensive strategy would involve a potential curtailment of the American people's freedoms and civil liberties. It would be subject to enemy reconnaissance and inevitable defeat. By contrast, an active, layered defense relies on early warning of an emerging threat in order to quickly deploy and execute a decisive response. This active defense is a powerful deterrent, dissuading adversaries and denying them any benefit from attacking the US homeland and imposing costs on those who attempt it.

The United States must keep potential adversaries off balance by both an effective defense of US territory and, when necessary, by projecting power across the globe. **We must seize the initiative from adversaries and apply all aspects of national power to deter, intercept, and disrupt attacks against us and our allies and friends. In short, the United States must act in ways that an enemy cannot predict, circumvent, or overcome.** Multiple barriers to attack must be deployed across the globe — in the forward regions, in the approaches to the United States, in the US homeland, and in the global commons — to create an unpredictable web of

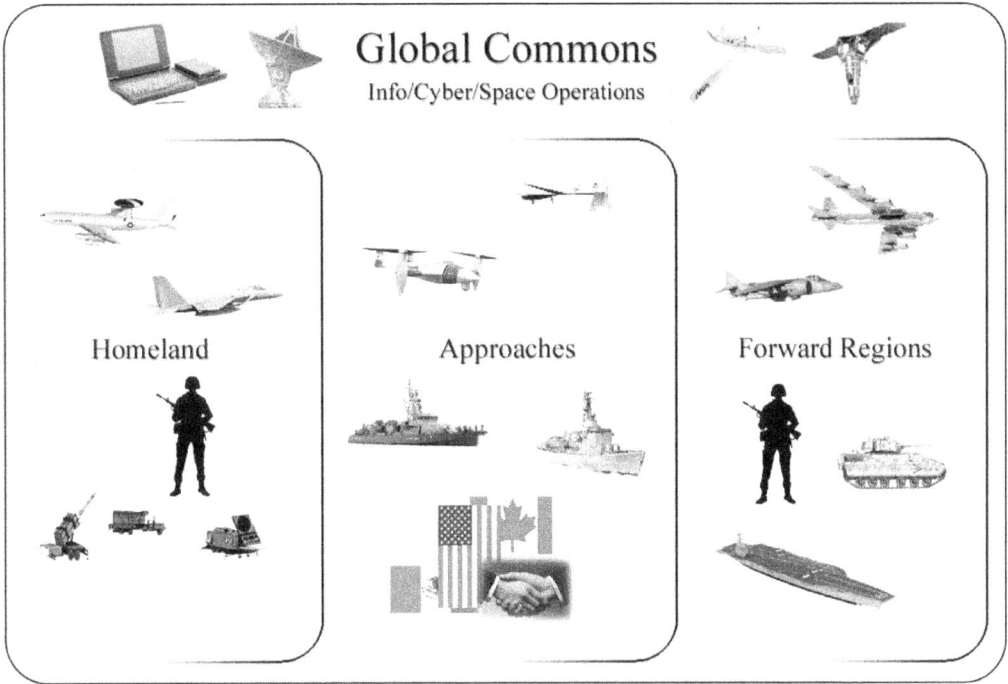

Figure 2: Active, Layered Defense Concept

land, maritime, and air assets that are arrayed to detect, deter, and defeat hostile action. When the United States identifies specific threats or vulnerabilities, it will strengthen deterrence through force projection, flexible deterrent options, heightened alert status, and tailored strategic communications.

The Forward Regions. The forward regions are foreign land areas, sovereign airspace, and sovereign waters outside the US homeland. The Department of Defense is a key contributor to the President's integrated national security effort abroad. To respond quickly to rising threats, the United States requires timely and actionable intelligence. Improved human intelligence (HUMINT) collection, improved intelligence integration and fusion, improved analysis of terrorist threats and targets, and improved technical collection against potential CBRNE weapons are all critical in this regard. In addition, the United States must counter and delegitimate

ideological support for terrorist groups, disrupt their flow of funding, and create an environment that curtails recruitment. US military forces must be trained, ready, and postured to intercept potential enemies, eliminate enemy sanctuaries, and maintain regional stability, in conjunction with allies and friendly states.

The Approaches. The land approaches to the continental United States are within the sovereign territory of Canada and Mexico. These nations, in close cooperation with the United States, contribute to North American security through their law enforcement, defense, and counterterrorism capabilities.

The waters and airspace geographically contiguous to the United States are critical homeland defense battlespaces. In these approaches, US Northern Command, the North American Aerospace Defense Command, and US Pacific Command,

11

working in concert with other combatant commands, the Intelligence Community, the US Coast Guard, and other domestic and international partners, have the opportunity to detect, deter, and, if necessary, defeat threats en route–before they reach the United States.[3] **This requires maximum awareness of threats in the approaches as well as the air and maritime interception capabilities necessary to maintain US freedom of action, secure the rights and obligations of the United States, and protect the nation at a safe distance.**

The US Homeland. The US homeland includes the United States, its territories and possessions, and the Commonwealths and Compact States of the Pacific. It also includes the surrounding territorial seas. Among its responsibilities within US territory, DoD focuses on the following areas:

- DoD is responsible for deterring and, when directed by the President, defeating direct attacks against the United States. NORAD is the cornerstone of our homeland air defense capability. Our air defense success rests on an integrated system for air surveillance and defense against air threats at all altitudes. DoD also maintains land forces capable of responding rapidly, when so directed, to threats against DoD personnel, defense critical infrastructure, or other domestic targets. Finally, DoD supports the US Coast Guard in the exercise of its maritime authorities under domestic and international law.

[3] The US Coast Guard is inherently flexible, as both a military service and law enforcement agency within the Department of Homeland Security. The US Coast Guard supports DoD in its homeland defense role, while DoD supports the Coast Guard in its homeland security role, across the forward regions, the global commons, the approaches, and within the US homeland.

- DoD supports civilian law enforcement and counterterrorism authorities consistent with US law. The Attorney General coordinates the activities of the law enforcement community to detect, prevent, preempt, and disrupt terrorist attacks against the United States. DoD support to the Department of Justice and other domestic law enforcement authorities includes providing expertise, intelligence, equipment, and training facilities to these authorities when so directed. It can also include the use of US military forces to support civilian law enforcement in responding to civil disturbances, as provided in US law.

- DoD provides critical CBRNE consequence management capabilities in support of civil authorities. With few exceptions, DoD's consequence management capabilities are designed for the wartime protection of the Department's personnel and facilities. Nevertheless, civil authorities are likely to call upon these capabilities if a domestic CBRNE catastrophe occurs in the ten-year period of this Strategy. **DoD must therefore equip and train these war-fighting forces, as necessary, for domestic CBRNE consequence management. Beyond an already dedicated command and control element designed for this purpose, however, DoD will continue to rely on dual-capable forces for domestic consequence management missions.**

The Global Commons. The global commons consist of international waters and airspace, space, and cyberspace. America's ability to deter threats against the global commons and to operate from them effectively is critical to the conduct of all its military missions, from the forward regions to the US homeland. Of particular note is the importance of space and cyberspace to US net-centric capabilities. **An active, layered defense requires a trustworthy information system, impervious to disabling digital or physical attacks.** Computer network defense must ensure that networks can self-diagnose problems and build immunity to future attacks. At the same time, networks must remain operational and consistently available for the execution of US military missions.

An active defense also requires the ability to detect and defeat threats from space. This includes the need for capable defenses against ballistic missiles. Ground facilities that support US military space systems are potential targets of attacks, and the Department will protect them.

III. Strategic Goal and Key Objectives

"We must build and maintain our defenses beyond challenge. Our military's highest priority is to defend the United States . . . The threats and enemies we must confront have changed, and so must our forces."

The National Security Strategy of the United States of America
September 2002

The employment of an active, layered defense across the globe is fundamental to achieving the Department of Defense's strategic goal for homeland defense. That is, **we will secure the United States from direct attack.** The National Defense Strategy emphasizes the Department of Defense's role in the forward regions and the global commons and how that role is critical to the defense of US territory. **This Strategy for Homeland Defense and Civil Support therefore focuses particular attention on the US homeland and its approaches.** In these geographic layers, the Department's activities to protect the United States generally fall into one of the following categories:

- *Lead:* DoD leads military missions to deter, prevent, and defeat attacks on the United States, its population, and its defense critical infrastructure. This includes defending the maritime and air approaches to the United States and protecting US airspace, territorial seas, and territory from attacks. The Department is also responsible for protecting DoD personnel located in US territory.

- *Support:* At the direction of the President or the Secretary of Defense, the Department provides defense support of civil authorities in order to prevent terrorist incidents or manage the consequences of an attack or a disaster. Civil authorities are most likely to request DoD support

where we have unique capabilities to contribute or when civilian responders are overwhelmed. DoD's contributions to the comprehensive national response effort can be critical, particularly in the near-term, as the Department of Homeland Security and other agencies strengthen their preparedness and response capabilities.

- *Enable:* Efforts to share capabilities and expertise with domestic agencies and international partners reinforce the Department's lead and support activities. At home, the Department works to improve civilian capabilities for homeland security by lending expertise and sharing relevant technology. For example, DoD is assisting the Department of Homeland Security in its efforts to develop intelligence analytical capabilities. We are also sharing training and simulation technologies, as well as unmanned aerial vehicle technologies for civilian surveillance along the Nation's borders. Abroad, the Department's security cooperation initiatives improve collective capabilities for homeland defense missions through exercises, information-sharing agreements, and formal defense agreements, such as NORAD.

To fulfill the key strategic goal of protecting the United States from attack, the Department of Defense will focus on achieving five key objectives directly related to the lead, support, and enable framework. In order of priority, these objectives are:

1. Achieve maximum awareness of potential threats (Lead);

2. Deter, intercept, and defeat threats at a safe distance from the United States, and US territories and possessions (Lead);

3. Achieve mission assurance (Lead);

4. Ensure DoD's ability to support civil authorities in domestic CBRNE consequence management (Support); and

5. Improve domestic and international partner capabilities for homeland defense and homeland security (Enable).

ACTIVITIES	OBJECTIVES	CORE CAPABILITIES
LEAD	Achieve Maximum Awareness of Threats	• Maintain agile and capable defense intelligence architecture • Analyze and understand potential threats • Detect, identify, and track emerging threats in all operational domains • Ensure shared situational awareness within DoD and with domestic and foreign partners
	Deter, Intercept, and Defeat Threats at a Safe Distance	• Deter adversaries from attacking the US homeland • Intercept and defeat national security threats in the maritime and air approaches and within US territory
	Achieve Mission Assurance	• Ensure force protection, to include DoD installations, especially against the threat of CBRNE attacks • Prepare and protect defense critical infrastructure • Ensure preparedness of the Defense Industrial Base • Prepare to protect designated national critical infrastructure • Ensure DoD crisis management and continuity preparedness
SUPPORT	Support Consequence Management for CBRNE Mass Casualty Attacks	• Manage consequences of CBRNE mass casualty attacks
ENABLE	Improve National and International Capabilities for Homeland Defense and Homeland Security	• Effective interagency planning and interoperability • Improved Federal, state, and local partnership capacity and effective domestic relationships • Improved international partnership capacity and effective defense-to-defense relationships

Figure 3: DoD Objectives and Core Capabilities for Protecting the United States from Attack

Lead

Objective 1: Achieve maximum awareness of threats

To defend the nation in the 21st century, the Department requires sufficient forewarning and immediate situational awareness of potential attacks. No longer is it sufficient to track the movement of hostile military aircraft and warships. In the 21st century threat environment, transnational terrorists and rogue states may employ a wide range of civilian vessels and aircraft as weapons, engage in cyber attacks, or target civilian infrastructure to achieve devastating effects.

To protect the United States in this environment, the Department of Defense, in cooperation with domestic and international partners, will seek to achieve maximum awareness of threats. By so doing, the United States increases the time available for an effective operational response. **Threat awareness includes the ability to obtain comprehensive, accurate, timely, and actionable intelligence and information; exploiting relevant information; and making it available to the warfighters, policy makers, and interagency and international partners responsible for identifying and responding to threats.**

An active, layered defense requires information to flow freely regardless of operational boundaries. Relevant information may originate in one or several of the operational domains—land, maritime, air, cyberspace, or space. It may originate from an array of domestic and foreign sources. To achieve maximum awareness of threats, information will be posted to DoD's Global Information Grid, integrating operational domains and facilitating information sharing across traditional military-civilian boundaries.

Objective 2: Deter, intercept, and defeat threats at a safe distance

During the Cold War, the United States focused on preventing Soviet submarines, ballistic missiles, and long-range bombers from attacking the American homeland. Although concerns about traditional conventional and nuclear threats to the US homeland remain, we recognize that in the next ten years, adversaries will present a host of new challenges. They may attempt to use commercial vessels to transport terrorists or weapons to the United States. They may attempt to intrude on US airspace with low-altitude aircraft, cruise missiles, and unmanned aerial vehicles. They may attempt to convert maritime vessels, aircraft, and other

modes of transportation into weapons. Through these and other means, our enemies will constantly employ asymmetric means to challenge the security of the United States.

In the maritime approaches, DoD is working with the Department of Homeland Security to integrate US maritime defense and to optimize the mutually supporting capabilities of the US Navy and the US Coast Guard. **As the Chief of Naval Operations (CNO) has stated, "forward deployed naval forces will network with other assets of the Navy and the Coast Guard, as well as the intelligence agencies to identify, track and intercept threats long before they threaten this nation."** This will require a level of situational awareness in the maritime domain similar to that in the air approaches. The goal, as the CNO explains, is to **"extend the security of the United States far seaward, taking advantage of the time and space purchased by forward deployed assets to protect the US from impending threats."**

In the air domain, DoD has primary responsibility for defending US airspace and protecting the United States from ballistic missiles, cruise missiles, and other aerospace attacks. For North America, this defense is carried out in partnership with Canada, through NORAD. In addition, the Department of Defense relies heavily on the Federal Aviation Administration (FAA) and the Department of Homeland Security (Transportation Security Administration) for early identification of air threats. As in the maritime environment, cooperation and operational coordination with our interagency partners, as well as our neighbors and other allies, is critical to protecting the United States from air threats.

Within US territory, we face the challenge of intercepting and defeating enemies determined to cause fear, death, and economic disruption. Although we must not dismiss traditional foreign military threats, in the period covered by this Strategy, domestic employment of the US military in a homeland defense role will likely come in response to transnational terrorist, rogue state, or other threats that exceed the capabilities of domestic counterterrorism and law enforcement authorities.

Therefore, the Department must approach the interception and defeat of threats to US territory from a joint, interagency, and, ultimately, intergovernmental perspective. DoD must not conduct operations in separate and distinct land, maritime, and air operational domains. Over the coming decade, US Northern Command, the North American Aerospace Defense Command, and US Pacific Command will continue to develop mature homeland defense capabilities in the air, land, and maritime domains, with appropriate support provided by other combatant commands.

Objective 3: Achieve mission assurance

The Department cannot fulfill any of the Strategy's key objectives without having the core capabilities in place to assure mission success. **Mission assurance, the certainty that DoD components can perform assigned tasks or duties in accordance with the intended purpose or plan, is therefore itself a key objective.** The Department of Defense achieves mission assurance through a range of programs and efforts that are aimed at securing DoD warfighting capabilities even when under attack or after disruption. These include force protection, the defense critical infrastructure program, and defense crisis management and continuity of operations efforts.

Force Protection. Force protection is central to achieving DoD mission assurance. It includes actions taken to prevent or mitigate hostile actions against DoD personnel (to include family members), resources, facilities, and critical information in an all hazards environment. Force protection measures can be defensive in nature, such as those used to reduce force and installation vulnerability to terrorist attacks or protect against CBRNE effects, or offensive, such as those taken to prevent, deter, and respond to terrorism. By conserving the force's fighting potential so that they can apply it at the decisive time and place, force protection ensures the effective employment of the joint force while degrading the enemy's opportunities.

An attack on DoD facilities could directly affect the Department's ability to project power overseas or carry out vital homeland defense functions. Installation commanders and facility managers have an inherent responsibility to protect the forces and installations under their command. Of particular concern is the threat to DoD personnel and installations posed by domestic CBRNE attacks.

CBRNE Preparedness. The Department of Defense will develop and implement a comprehensive preparedness plan for CBRNE attacks. This plan will leverage capabilities and programs throughout the Department (e.g. Critical Infrastructure Protection, Antiterrorism/Force Protection, Project Guardian) including required intelligence support. In accordance with DoD responsibilities in National Biodefense Policy, the Department is especially attentive to the unique challenges posed by biological agents.

Defense Critical Infrastructure. Related to its force protection responsibilities for DoD facilities, the Department of Defense has the responsibility to assure it has access to *defense critical infrastructure.* This is defined as DoD and non-DoD cyber and physical assets and associated infrastructure essential to project and support military forces worldwide. When these infrastructures are located on Department of Defense installations, their protection is the responsibility of the installation commander or facility manager. In some instances, however, critical defense assets are located at public or private sites beyond the direct control of DoD. In either case, the protection of designated defense critical infrastructure must be assured on a priority basis.

In some scenarios, assurance of non-DoD infrastructures might involve protection activities, in close coordination with other Federal, state, local, tribal, or private sector partners. This could include elements of the Defense Industrial Base, which is a world-wide industrial complex with capabilities to perform research and development and design, produce, and maintain military weapons systems, subsystems, components, or parts to meet military requirements. These defense-related products and services are essential to mobilize, deploy, and sustain military operations. Moreover, defense critical infrastructure could also include selected civil and commercial infrastructures that provide the power, communications, transportation, and other utilities that military forces and DoD support organizations rely on to meet their operational needs.

In addition, the President or the Secretary of Defense might direct US military forces to protect non-DoD assets of national signifi-cance that are so vital to the nation that their

incapacitation could have a debilitating effect on the security of the United States.

Defense Crisis Management and Continuity of Operations. During an emergency, the nation's leaders, including DoD decision-makers, must be able to carry out vital government functions. **The Department must provide the President and Secretary of Defense with survivable and enduring national command and control of DoD assets and US military forces.** DoD also plays an important supporting role in ensuring Continuity of Government and Enduring Constitutional Government in times of crisis. In the Cold War era, DoD continuity efforts focused on survival of senior leadership to prosecute war in the aftermath of a massive nuclear attack. Today, DoD's crisis manage-ment efforts are broader, responsive to the full range of potential threats to the nation. Meeting the Department's crisis management objectives requires ready DoD transportation assets, capable and survivable remote operation sites, and advanced communi-cations capabilities throughout the DoD continuity architecture.

Support

Objective 4: Support consequence management for CBRNE mass-casualty attacks

The Department has traditionally supported civil authorities in a wide variety of domestic contingencies, usually natural disasters. DoD typically does so using military forces and DoD capabilities designed for use in expedi-tionary warfighting missions. That support continues today. For example, unique national intelligence capabilities located within the Defense intelligence community continuously support other US Government agencies. Although these traditional types of defense support of civil authorities are likely to continue, they are not likely to impede DoD's ability to execute other missions specified in the National Defense Strategy.

At the high end of the threat spectrum, however, the 21st century environment has fundamentally altered the terms under which Department of Defense assets and capabilities might be called upon for support. **The potential for multiple, simultaneous, CBRNE attacks on US territory is real.** It is therefore imperative that the Department of Defense be prepared to support civilian responders in responding to such mass casualty events.

Support to domestic authorities for consequence management is a core element of active, layered defense. The Department of Defense maintains considerable CBRNE recovery expertise and equipment. When directed by the President or the Secretary of Defense, DoD will employ these capabilities to assist the Secretary of Homeland Security, the principal Federal official for domestic incident management, or other domestic authorities. DoD must be prepared to support its interagency partners in responding to a range of CBRNE incidents, including multiple, simultaneous mass casualty attacks within the United States.

Enable

Objective 5: Improve national and international capabilities for homeland defense and homeland security

The broad range of threats posed by terrorists and other transnational actors has expanded our traditional concept of national security. In the past, the Department of Defense could largely fulfill its responsibility for protecting the nation by integrating its activities with the Department of State and the Intelligence Community. Today, the expertise and responsibility for managing security challenges is much more widely shared among Federal departments and agencies. State, local, and tribal authorities, the private sector, and our allies and friends abroad are also critical contributors to US national security.

In such an environment, DoD must unify its efforts with those of its key interagency partners and international friends and allies to ensure the nation's security. The Department will promote the integration and sharing of applicable DoD capabilities, equipment, and technologies with Federal, state, local, and tribal authorities and the private sector. Sharing technology, capabilities, and expertise strengthens the nation's ability to respond to hostile threats and domestic emergencies. Likewise, cooperative homeland defense education and training initiatives will help partners build capacity for homeland defense and will foster a common understanding of shared threats and how best to address them. In turn, DoD can readily leverage the expertise of other Federal, state, local, and tribal authorities and international partners to improve its own capabilities for counterterrorism, maritime interception, and other missions critical to an active, layered defense.

IV. Core Capabilities

"Some believe that, with the U.S. in the midst of a dangerous war on terrorism, now is not the time to transform our armed forces. I believe that quite the opposite is true. Now is precisely the time to make changes. The impetus and the urgency added by the events of September 11th powerfully make the case for action."

Secretary of Defense Donald Rumsfeld

January 31, 2002

The Department of Defense will provide the homeland defense and civil support capabilities necessary to support implementation of the National Security Strategy, the National Strategy for Homeland Security, and the National Defense Strategy. Over the next ten years, DoD will protect the United States from attack by developing the core capabilities necessary to achieve each of the key objectives detailed in Section III.

Capabilities for Achieving Maximum Awareness of Threats

Core Capability: Capable and agile defense intelligence architecture

Protecting the United States against the full-range of 21st century threats requires the US Intelligence Community to restore its human intelligence capabilities, reprioritize intelligence collection to address probable homeland defense threats, and continue to invest in intelligence, reconnaissance, and surveillance (ISR) sensor capabilities. In the Cold War, we knew both the nature of the threat to our country and the source of that threat. Today, intelligence and warning must extend beyond conventional military and strategic nuclear threats to cover a wide range of other state and non-state challenges that may manifest themselves overseas or at home.

The Intelligence Community is adjusting to this changing strategic landscape to meet the nation's homeland security needs. The establishment of a National Intelligence Director, the National Counterterrorism Center (NCTC), the Department of Homeland Security's Information Analysis and Infrastructure Protection Directorate, and the DoD's Joint Intelligence Task Force for Combating Terrorism (JITF-CT) exemplifies this shift. Executive Orders for strengthened management of the Intelligence Community also ensure a more collaborative, comprehensive approach to intelligence support for national security. While these changes are taking place, the Department of Defense is reorienting its intelligence capabilities in line with the full range of homeland defense priorities. Specifically, the Department will:

- Focus on integrated collection management of foreign and military information and its application to homeland defense and homeland security;

- Better utilize national intelligence capabilities to increase early warning and support prevention, interception, and disruption of potential threats overseas or in the approaches to the United States;

- Collect homeland defense threat information from relevant private and public sector sources, consistent with US constitutional authorities and privacy law;

- Identify capability needs for CBRNE sensors to meet homeland defense requirements; and

- Develop automated tools to improve data fusion, analysis, and management, to track systematically large amounts of data, and to detect, fuse, and analyze aberrant patterns of activity, consistent with US privacy protections.

Core Capability: Collect, analyze, and understand potential threats

Improving our understanding of America's foreign enemies—in advance of an attack—is at the heart of DoD's efforts to achieve maximum awareness of potential threats. In accordance with the National Strategy for Combating Terrorism (2002), we are strengthening DoD's knowledge of foreign terrorist networks and the inner workings of their operations.

Improved human intelligence, particularly in the forward regions of the world, is the single most important factor in understanding terrorist organizations. The Department of Defense is currently undertaking a focused review of DoD human intelligence capabilities, including reforms to improve HUMINT career development, policies, practices, and organizations. DoD HUMINT operators must have relevant linguistic skills and cultural understanding as well as the technical skills needed to provide high-quality information to the analysts.

In addition, we will **develop a cadre of specialized terrorism intelligence analysts within the Defense intelligence community** and deploy a number of these analysts to interagency centers for homeland defense and counterterrorism analysis and operations. The Department will maintain significant counterterrorism collection and analytical capability to support military activities overseas and in the approaches to the United States.

National agencies within the Department, such as the National Security Agency and the National Geospatial-Intelligence Agency, will continue to provide their unique capabilities in support of the national homeland security mission in accordance with applicable laws and regulations. The Department will also maintain an analytical capability to identify threats to defense critical infrastructure.

Core Capability: Detection, identification, and tracking of emerging threats in all operational domains

We face challenges in our ability to detect, identify, and track objects in all operational environments. Every day, thousands of US and foreign vessels and aircraft approach and depart North American ports and airports, and many times that number of individuals and vehicles cross our borders. For the Department of Defense, these challenges are especially pertinent in the air and maritime domains, where the military plays a much more substantial role.

To detect and track anticipated air and maritime threats effectively, the United States must have capabilities to cue, surveil, identify, engage, and assess potential threats in real time. Detection and tracking capabilities must be all-weather, around-the-clock, and effective against moving targets. The United States must also have the ability to detect CBRNE threats emanating from any operating environment. **This requires a**

21

comprehensive, all-domain CBRNE detection architecture, from collection to dissemination.

The maritime domain is multi-jurisdictional, with various US agencies responsible for tracking vessels from their departure at foreign ports to their arrival in the United States. Recognizing the potential vulnerability this situation creates, DoD is working closely with interagency partners, especially the Department of Homeland Security, to finalize a unified concept for maritime domain awareness (MDA)—the effective understanding of anything associated with the global maritime domain that could affect the security, safety, economy, or environment of the United States. The purpose of MDA is to facilitate timely, accurate decision-making.

Based on the emerging MDA concept and related efforts that will result from the implementation of National Security Presidential Directive-41/Homeland Security Presidential Directive-13: National Maritime Security, the Department of Defense will work with interagency partners to develop a comprehensive capability to detect threats as far forward of the US homeland as possible, ideally before threat vessels depart foreign ports. **DoD will ensure persistent wide-area surveillance and reconnaissance of the US maritime approaches, layered and periodically varied in such a manner that an adversary cannot predict or evade observation.** The nation will benefit from the Department of Homeland Security's work to institute worldwide cargo and crew reliability mechanisms. DoD, in concert with the Department of Homeland Security, will receive and share data from improved identification systems for small commercial and other vessels, just as it has done for

maritime vessels of over 300 gross tons that are on international voyages.

Achieving threat awareness in the air operational domain presents similar challenges. Throughout the Cold War, the Department of Defense focused on maintaining awareness of external threats that entered US airspace from overseas. The attacks on September 11, 2001, however, originated in US airspace and highlighted weaknesses in domestic radar coverage and interagency air defense coordination. Adversaries might maintain low altitude flight profiles, employ stealth and other defense countermeasures, or engage in deception to challenge US air defenses.

Since the attacks of September 11, 2001, DoD has coordinated with interagency partners to improve significantly the air defense of the United States. DoD has worked with the Federal Aviation Administration to integrate domestic radar coverage and has conducted Operation Noble Eagle air patrols to protect designated US cities and critical assets. We have placed particular emphasis on implementing a robust air defense capability for the National Capital Region, using both air and ground air defense forces.

The Department of Defense will continue to work with domestic and international partners to develop a persistent, wide-area surveillance and reconnaissance capability for the airspace within US borders, as well as over the nation's approaches. This capability could require the development of advanced technology sensors to detect and track low-altitude air vehicles across a wide geographic area. DoD is investigating various technologies that could provide an over-the-horizon engagement capability to detect enemy threats in the approaches or over US territory. The United States and our allies must also integrate sensor and intelligence data to identify hostile air vehicles by observing their performance characteristics, suspicious activities, or other attributes. These capabilities in the air domain will provide timely threat detection, extending the depth of air defenses and the time for response, thereby providing multiple engagement opportunities to defeat identified threats.

Core Capability: Shared situational awareness within DoD and with domestic and foreign partners

Shared situational awareness is defined as a common perception of the environment and its implications. All domestic and foreign partners within the homeland defense mission space require situational awareness for three reasons: to identify threats as early and as distant from US borders as possible; to provide ample time for an optimal course of action; and to allow for a flexible operational response. From the March 2003 Homeland Security Information Sharing Memorandum of Agreement, to the aggressive and unprecedented information sharing underway at the NCTC, the US Government continues to make great strides in overcoming obstacles to shared situational awareness.

During the Cold War, the Department of Defense sought shared situational awareness with the Department of State, the Intelligence Community, and allied nations to deter and defeat threats posed by the Soviet Union and other nations. At the same time, the American law enforcement community worked with its international counterparts to thwart international drug cartels and worldwide crime syndicates.

Today, transnational terrorists have blurred the traditional distinction between national security and international law enforcement. Together with the development of other security threats, **this expanded national security challenge necessitates an unprecedented degree of shared situational awareness among Federal agencies, with state, local, tribal, and private entities, and between the United States and its key foreign partners.**

As a first step, the Department of Defense must provide seamless connectivity and timely, accurate, and trusted information to all DoD Components—any time, any place—to achieve maximum awareness of potential attacks against the United States. The Department will therefore ensure that DoD's information infrastructure provides an integrated, interoperable worldwide network of information technology products and management services. This will allow users across DoD to process information and move it to warfighters, policymakers, and support personnel on demand. Network connectivity must be flexible enough to support global operations while allowing for local requirements and innovation. **It must also create a real-time link among sensors, decision makers, and warfighters to facilitate the rapid engagement of enemy targets.**

Beyond building an integrated information infrastructure, DoD must also populate that network with accurate, timely, and actionable data. Today, information relevant to protecting the United States is widely dispersed. The Department, in concert with the intelligence and law enforcement communities and foreign partners, will build on the great strides already made to diminish existing cultural, technological, and bureaucratic obstacles to information sharing. The

Intelligence Community and Department of Defense will drive improved information sharing within a "need to share" context. The resulting information exchange, commonly referred to as "horizontal integration of intelligence," will provide analysts across the US Government and partner nations with timely and accurate all-source information, vastly improving the creation of a coherent and fully integrated threat picture. Such an expansion in information sharing requires appropriate safeguards to ensure that DoD intelligence components rigorously apply laws that protect Americans' civil liberties and privacy.

Capabilities for Deterring, Intercepting, and Defeating Threats at a Safe Distance

Core Capability: Deter adversaries from attacking the US homeland.

DoD's efforts to secure the United States from direct attack are intrinsically linked to the concept of deterrence. The objective of deterrence is to convince potential adversaries that threatening courses of action will result in outcomes decisively worse than they could achieve through other, non-threatening, means.

Just as the range of potential adversaries of the United States varies, so, too, do the most effective means of deterrence. Generally, however, our deterrent is enabled by global situational awareness, effective command and control, military presence abroad, the strength and agility of US military forces, strong domestic and international cooperation and sustained global influence, and a coherent national strategic communications campaign. Information operations, influence operations, control of the operational domains, conventional and nuclear global strike capabilities, and active and passive defense measures all contribute significantly to deterring threats to the US homeland.

Core Capability: Interception and defeat of national security threats in the maritime and air approaches and within US territory

Maritime Operational Domain. The United States must be able to detect terrorists on the high seas armed with weapons of mass destruction. Accordingly, we will fully integrate our surface, subsurface, air, and surveillance assets, focus them forward, and identify, track and intercept threats at a safe distance from the US. In so doing, we will work with our domestic and international partners and take action consistent with applicable law.

Improving our ability to intercept enemies in the maritime domain requires an integrated system of overlapping defenses—both adaptable and flexible—to frustrate enemy observation and avoid predictability. This begins in the forward regions with improved surveillance capability, increased HUMINT collection, and strengthened international partnerships through programs like the Container Security Initiative and Proliferation Security Initiative. To maximize maritime domain awareness, successive layers of surveillance must be fully coordinated with the operational activity of our forward deployed forces.

DoD has established standing orders for conducting maritime homeland defense and maritime interception operations. Given this guidance, geographic combatant commanders will include interception exercises in their security cooperation plans and conduct such exercises on a periodic basis. The US Navy and US Coast Guard will conduct routine and frequent maritime interception exercises to ensure a high state of readiness.

To intercept and defeat transnational threats, the Department of Defense and Department of Homeland Security must have a predetermined process for ensuring rapid, effective US Coast Guard support to the US Navy and vice versa. Although DoD has the lead role in defending the United States from direct maritime attack, we recognize and support the US Coast Guard's responsibilities for maritime law enforcement and homeland security. Together with the US Coast Guard, we must strengthen the security in our ports and littorals, expanding maritime defense capabilities further seaward.

The United States must have a concept of operations for the active, layered maritime defense of the US homeland. Such a concept will require naval forces be responsive to US Northern Command, consistent with maritime mission requirements, and will require that Navy forces be placed under periodic command and control of US Northern Command as appropriate. DoD will also consider the use of US Naval Reserve forces to undertake unique roles in maritime homeland defense. In addition, the US Navy should assess how forces currently used in support of Operation Noble Eagle, together with available coastal patrol craft and future Naval and Joint capabilities, such as the Navy's littoral combat ship, might be used to execute maritime homeland defense missions.

Air Operational Domain. The Department of Defense will defeat air threats to the United States, such as ballistic and cruise missiles

and attacking military aircraft. DoD must also be prepared to intercept non-traditional air threats, even when the intent to harm the United States is uncertain, as initially occurred on September 11, 2001. These threats could include commercial or chartered aircraft, general aviation, ultralight airplanes, unmanned aerial vehicles, radio controlled aircraft, or even balloons. Early detection and successful interception of these types of potential threats requires very close cooperation with DoD's interagency partners.

Since September 11, 2001, the Department of Defense, through Operation Noble Eagle, has conducted air patrols to protect major US population centers, critical infrastructure, and other sites. Working with our interagency partners, DoD will continue these patrols to intercept air threats to the US homeland as long as required.

The Department of Defense will continue to improve the air-to-air and ground-to-air capabilities and associated forces necessary to intercept and defeat all domestic air threats. For air patrol missions, DoD will use more capable aircraft as they are fielded and explore the potential for employing unmanned combat air vehicles. DoD is also upgrading ground-based air defense assets with improved detection and targeting capabilities.

The Department of Defense will devote significant attention to defending US territory against cruise missile attacks. Defense against cruise missiles poses unique challenges, given that their low altitude and small size make them more difficult to identify and track than traditional air threats. The Department of Defense is developing integrated capabilities to defend against cruise missiles, as well as other types of unmanned aerial vehicles. As an interim step, DoD is developing a deployable air and cruise missile defense capability to protect designated areas. This capability aims to integrate Service tactical air defense assets, the NORAD air defense system, interagency information sources, and advanced technology sensors. **Future air and cruise missile defense assets will be fully interoperable, increase the size of the defended area, and engage threats at increased range.**

DoD will also continue to work with interagency partners to develop a common air surveillance picture that will improve our ability to identify and, ultimately, defeat enemy targets. An improved capability is required to detect and track potential air threats within the United States. The current radars maintained by the Federal Aviation Administration to track air traffic within the United States are aging, with high maintenance costs, poor reliability, and reduced capability to track emerging threats. **The nation will need to develop an advanced capability to replace the current generation of radars to improve tracking and identification of low-altitude threats.**

Land Operational Domain. The Department of Defense will be prepared to detect, deter and defeat direct, land-based attacks conducted by hostile nations against the United States. When directed by the President, the Department will execute land-based military operations to detect, deter, and defeat foreign terrorist attacks within the United States. To achieve these mission requirements, we must work closely with our neighbors, establish seamless relationships and organizational structures with interagency partners, and be prepared to respond with military forces on our own soil quickly, responsively, and in a manner that is well coordinated with civilian law enforcement agencies.

Historically, the United States relied almost exclusively on forward deployed forces to confront and defeat nation-state adversaries overseas. Although military power projection remains crucial, transnational terrorism has significantly reduced the effectiveness of this singular approach. Now and in the future, we must be prepared in every part of the globe—most especially the US homeland—to deter, prevent, and defeat terrorist or other asymmetric threats.

The employment of military forces to conduct missions on US territory is constrained by law and historic public policy. It is the primary mission of the Department of Homeland Security to prevent terrorist attacks within the United States. The Attorney General leads our Nation's law enforcement effort to detect, prevent, and investigate terrorist activity within the United States. The scope of DoD's role in preventing terrorist attacks within the US land domain is defined by the President's constitutional authority as Commander in Chief and limited by statutory authority related to military support of civilian law enforcement. Domestic security is primarily a civilian law enforcement function.

The following three-tiered approach provides the parameters under which the military would likely operate:

Tier 1: Local and Federal law enforcement. When directed by the President or the Secretary of Defense, DoD will provide appropriate defense assets in support of domestic law enforcement authority, normally in support of a lead Federal agency such as the FBI. Under these circumstances, military forces and assets will remain under the command and control of DoD.

Tier 2: National Guard forces not on Federal Active Duty. When directed by the Governor or appropriate state authority, National Guard forces and assets in state active duty status can respond quickly to perform homeland defense and homeland security activities within US territory.

Newly expanded authorities under Title 32 of US Code—and the National Guard's on-going transformation—provide Governors and state authorities with the authority to use flexible, responsive National Guard units for a limited period to perform homeland defense activities, when approved by the Secretary of Defense. For example, National Guard forces may, when the Secretary of Defense determines that doing so is both necessary and appropriate, provide security for critical infrastructure and support civilian law enforcement agencies in responding to terrorist acts.

Tier 3: US military forces responding to Presidential direction. If circumstances warrant, the President or the Secretary of Defense may direct military forces and assets to intercept and defeat threats on US territory. **When conducting land defense missions on US territory, DoD does so as a core, warfighting mission, fulfilling the Commander in Chief's Constitutional obligation to defend the nation.** To fulfill this responsibility, DoD will ensure the availability of appropriately sized, trained, equipped, and ready forces. Currently, this capability is provided by quick reaction forces (QRFs) and rapid reaction forces (RRFs).

Capabilities for Achieving Mission Assurance

Core Capability: Ensure Force Protection

As previously noted, force protection is that set of measures taken to prevent or mitigate hostile actions against Department of Defense personnel (to include family members), resources, facilities, and critical information. The Department of Defense has institutionalized force protection as a core capability across the Services to lessen the adverse effects of incidents, whether man-made or natural, on key infrastructure within DoD installations and facilities.

CBRNE Preparedness. Although force protection is an all-hazards concept, the Department is particularly concerned about the threat that adversary use of CBRNE poses to DoD personnel and installations. Improving DoD's capabilities for mitigating and, if necessary, operating in a CBRNE-contaminated environment will require progress in detecting and identifying threats (sense), providing early warning (shape), protecting forces and installations (shield), and ensuring the ability to operate in a contaminated environment (sustain). DoD's Joint Chemical and Biological Defense Program is focused on developing and fielding technologies to mitigate, and if necessary, to allow forces to operate in, CBRNE contaminated environments.

   Sense. DoD currently has a range of capabilities to detect, identify, and quantify airborne, waterborne, and other hazards. Needed improvements include advanced standoff and point detection

27

capabilities for chemical and biological threats. DoD is also working to develop and field standoff detection capabilities for explosives. Advances in standoff detection capability will improve the Department's ability to detect nuclear devices as well as weapons using explosives to disperse chemical, biological, and radioactive materials. Finally, the Department is improving medical surveillance capabilities both on installations and within surrounding communities to provide early detection and identification of CBRNE events in the workforce.

Shape. DoD characterizes CBRNE attacks by assimilating information drawn from sensors, hazard prediction models, and elsewhere to inform commanders of impending or approaching threats. The Department is improving on early CBRNE threat characterization by developing an integrated concept of operations for sensing, reporting, and warning of CBRNE attacks, and ensuring compatibility with national-level CBRNE sensor architectures, such as the Department of Homeland Security's BIOWATCH program.

Shield. The Department will continue to provide force protection in advance of a potential CBRNE attack, whether overseas or at domestic installations. Already, more than 850,000 US military personnel have been vaccinated against anthrax; more than 730,000 are vaccinated against smallpox. The Department is now focusing on the development of vaccines and other capabilities that can address new and emerging biological and chemical threats. This includes significant research on technologies for improved

chemical and biological agent detection and personal and collective protection equipment. DoD is also preparing to field capabilities that protect US forces from chemical agents that can be absorbed through the skin.

Lastly, the Department is deepening and expanding collaboration on biodefense research with the Department of Homeland Security and the Department of Health and Human Services. This includes significant new investments by these civilian agencies and the creation of a new research consortium. The construction of a National Interagency Biodefense Campus, collocated with the US Army Medical Research Institute of Infectious Diseases (USAMRIID), will significantly facilitate civil-military cooperation in this area. A revitalized and recapitalized USAMRIID, along with major Department of Homeland Security and Department of Health and Human Services investments, will provide DoD and the nation with added research capacity, additional biopharmaceutical development, increased testing and evaluation of potential biodefense medical products, and large surge lab capacity for bioterrorism incident response.

Sustain. DoD must be able to sustain operations during and after a CBRNE attack in the United States. Medical therapeutics that allow DoD personnel to continue mission-essential tasks in a CBRNE environment are of highest priority. DoD will also expand pilot programs for CBRNE installation preparedness to protect DoD personnel and facilities in the event of an attack. In addition to providing improved CBRNE defense capabilities at 200 critical installations in the United States and abroad through the Guardian Program, DoD will improve its capability to protect all installations through updated doctrine and guidance. The Department will examine an aggressive expansion of force protection and related programs to increase both the level of protection and the number of DoD installations it covers.

Core Capability: Preparedness and protection of defense critical infrastructure

Because resources are constrained, uniform protection of all defense critical infrastructure is not possible. **The Department must prioritize the protection of assets based on their criticality to executing the National Defense Strategy and seek to minimize the vulnerability of critical assets in accordance with integrated risk management approach.** To this end, the Department will devise a strategy to:

- Identify infrastructure critical to the accomplishment of DoD missions, based on a mission area analysis.

- Assess the potential effect of a loss or degradation of critical infrastructure on DoD operations to determine specific vulnerabilities, especially from terrorist attack.

- Manage the risk of loss, degradation, or disruption of critical assets through remediation or mitigation efforts, such as changes in tactics, techniques, and procedures; minimizing single points of service; and creating appropriate redundancies, where feasible.

- Protect infrastructure at the direction of the President or the Secretary of Defense where the nature of the threat exceeds the

capabilities of an asset owner and civilian law enforcement is insufficient.

- Enable real-time incident management operations by integrating current threat data and relevant critical infrastructure requirements.

The Military Departments, Defense Agencies, and other DoD components are now implementing the Protective Risk Management Strategy through modifications to their programs and budgets.

Core Capability: Preparedness of the Defense Industrial Base

The National Strategy for the Physical Protection of Critical Infrastructure and Key Assets (2003) notes that, **without the important contributions of the private sector, DoD cannot effectively execute core defense missions.** Private industry manufactures and provides the majority of the equipment, materials, services, and weapons for the US armed forces. The President recently designated DoD as the Sector-Specific Agency for the Defense Industrial Base (DIB). **In this role, DoD is responsible for national infrastructure protection activities for critical defense industries as set forth in Homeland Security Presidential Directive-7.**

To assure that mission critical supplies and services are available, DoD contracts are being modified to ensure that protective measures are in place at key facilities and that DoD can assess the security of the DIB. In addition, the Defense Logistics Agency and other DoD contracting activities are revising the contract process to ensure that civilian defense contractors are able to operate for the duration of a national emergency. **Defense contractors must be able to maintain**

adequate response times, ensure supply and labor availability, and provide direct logistic support in times of crisis. DoD program managers will be held accountable for ensuring the protection of supporting infrastructure, including key suppliers. DoD base and installation commanders, and those who contract for non-DoD infrastructure services and assets, will monitor assurance activities through compliance with contract language that clearly identifies reliable service availability, priority of restoration, and asset protection.

Core Capability: Preparedness to protect designated national critical infrastructure

The Department has historically focused on preventing unauthorized personnel from gaining access to DoD installations and protecting those installations from traditional military attacks. **In the post-September 11, 2001 era, DoD is expanding the traditional concept of critical asset protection to include protection from acts of transnational terrorism.** Countering terrorist reconnaissance activity is central to the successful defense of critical infrastructure.

As outlined in the National Strategy for the Physical Protection of Critical Infrastructures and Key Assets (2003), DoD bears responsibility for protecting its own assets, infrastructure, and personnel. At the Department's request, domestic law enforcement may protect DoD facilities.

For non-DoD infrastructure, including private and public assets that are critical to the execution of the National Defense Strategy, DoD's protection role is more limited. The initial responsibility for protection of non-DoD infrastructure rests with asset owners.

Civilian law enforcement authorities augment and reinforce the efforts of asset owners, creating a second tier of protection.

Should protection requirements exceed the capabilities of asset owners and civilian law enforcement, state authorities provide an additional layer of defense. In addition to a Governor's authority to employ National Guard forces in a state active duty status, recent changes to Title 32 of the US Code may provide an additional, expeditious means to use National Guard forces under the control of the Governor, with the approval of the Secretary of Defense, using Federal funding to perform homeland defense activities.

To achieve critical infrastructure protection in the most serious situations, the Department of Defense maintains trained and ready combat forces for homeland defense missions.

Core Capability: Defense crisis management and DoD continuity preparedness

The Department's crisis management and continuity of operations programs are central to mission assurance. DoD must provide capabilities necessary to support senior leadership decision-making and military command and control and to perform essential DoD functions to support national-level crisis managers. DoD is working to strengthen its information management and communications capabilities to support senior leadership in crises. It is also improving the survivability and flexibility of military command and control capabilities.

A significant element of mission assurance is **continuity of operations**—maintaining the ability to carry out DoD mission essential functions in the event of a national emergency or terrorist attack. Fulfilling this objective in the current security environment necessitates new and innovative approaches, such as improving policies for personnel dispersion, leveraging information technology to improve crisis coordination, and improving relocation facilities. The Department recently conducted a zero-based assessment of DoD continuity capabilities. The results of this assessment detail numerous capability improvements that the Department can pursue to ensure the continuity of DoD operations in times of crisis. It will transform DoD's approach to continuity operations from a Cold War-oriented concept to one better suited to the terrorist threat.

Capabilities for CBRNE Consequence Management

Core Capability: Consequence management assistance for domestic CBRNE mass casualty attacks

The Department of Defense must be able to conduct major operations in a CBRNE environment. US military forces organize, train, and equip to operate in contaminated environments, as well as manage the consequences of CBRNE incidents, on a level unmatched by any other single domestic agency or international partner. **If directed by the President or the Secretary of Defense, the Department of Defense must be prepared to use these capabilities to assist interagency partners in the aftermath of domestic CBRNE mass casualty attacks.** DoD's CBRNE capabilities include specialized agent detection, identification, and dispersion modeling systems as well as casualty extraction and mass decontamination abilities. DoD can also provide significant support to domestic consequence

management by providing emergency medical support, such as equipment, mobile hospitals, aeromedical evacuation, medical personnel, engineering support, and mortuary services.

Not all domestic CBRNE incidents will necessitate a Federal response; many scenarios may be well within the capabilities of state and local responders. Those incidents that do require a US Government response will be coordinated by a lead Federal agency. In most catastrophic scenarios, DoD will be called upon to provide support to the Department of Homeland Security or another Federal agency. **The Department will work closely with interagency partners—through the National Response Plan and the National Incident Management System—to ensure proficiency and interoperability in responding to multiple CBRNE incidents.**

The Department will ensure that dedicated CBRNE civil support capabilities are sized, trained, equipped, and ready for the domestic consequence management mission. Dedicated domestic CBRNE command and control is provided by the Joint Task Force-Civil Support. In addition, the National Guard WMD Civil Support Teams can operate under Federal control in times of crisis, when directed to do so by the President or Secretary of Defense. DoD is currently examining the augmentation of WMD Civil Support Teams with National Guard and other military capabilities and forces that are task-organized for this mission.

DoD will also identify, train, and equip an additional, discrete number of military forces for the potential requirements associated with multiple, simultaneous CBRNE attacks within the United States. These forces will be dual-mission in nature—these warfighters and support elements will not be dedicated to the civil support role but they will nevertheless be ready to perform domestic consequence management missions when required.[4]

Lastly, the Department will ensure that other elements of the Total Force—currently sized and shaped primarily for overseas missions—are identified, exercised, and ready to support CBRNE consequence management as necessary. This capability will provide added utility for overseas deployments or domestic missions. Within this Total Force context, DoD's effectiveness in responding to domestic CBRNE contingencies will be greatly improved through adjustments to Active and Reserve Component training, procedures that allow for faster mobilization of National Guard and Reserve Forces, and improved command relationships that make optimal use of the Reserve Component. This includes leveraging the National Guard's proposed Joint Force Headquarters-State organizations.

---

[4] Among existing dual-use DoD assets are the US Marine Corps Chemical-Biological Incident Response Force (CBIRF); the US Army Technical Escort Unit; the US Army Chemical Biological Rapid Response Team; the Defense Threat Reduction Agency's Consequence Management Advisory Team; the US Army 52nd Ordinance Group; the US Navy Environmental and Preventive Medicine Unit; the US Naval Medical Research Center; the US Navy Defense Technical Response Group; the US Air Force Radiation Assessment Team; and the US Air Force Technical Application Center.

Improving US and International Capabilities for Homeland Defense and Homeland Security

Core Capability: Interagency planning and interoperability

Recognizing the critical importance of interoperability, DoD will share training, planning, and other appropriate resources with interagency partners to standardize operational concepts, develop technology requirements, and coordinate budget planning for homeland missions. Interagency efforts must focus on closing any remaining seams in air, land, maritime, cyberspace and space operational domains and must improve national preparedness and incident management efforts. Development of a coordinated training and exercise program is an essential step toward greater cooperation in executing homeland defense and civil support missions.

Active DoD participation in the interagency process improves planning and interoperability and will ensure that procedures for supporting civil authorities are consistent with the framework for domestic incident response outlined in the National Response Plan and the National Incident Management System.

Core Capability: Improved Federal, state, and local partnership capacity and effective domestic relationships

The Department of Defense has identified three tenets to improve defense support of civil authorities:

- Augment civil capabilities with DoD expertise where necessary;

- Ensure the seamless operational integration of defense support capabilities with those of the civil sector;

- Assist in the civil sector's development and procurement of new technologies and equipment.

Within this civil support framework, the Department will actively seek to identify opportunities for cooperation with the civil sector. Several initiatives to strengthen civilian capabilities are already underway. Examples include:

- DoD assistance to the Department of Homeland Security to develop CBRNE victim rescue capabilities, similar to those of the US Marine Corps' Chemical Biological Incident Response Force.

- Joint DoD and Department of Homeland Security research and development on, and civilian acquisition of unmanned aerial vehicles for law enforcement and ground surveillance systems for border security.

- DoD efforts through the Interagency Counter Man-Portable Air Defense System (MANPADS) Task Force to help develop an attack prevention and recovery plan, provide technical advice and analysis to the Department of Homeland Security regarding MANPADS countermeasures, and operational assistance to stem the proliferation of MANPADS overseas.

In compliance with Section 1401 of the National Defense Authorization Act for FY 2003, DoD will continue efforts to transfer competencies between DoD and the civil sector—through technology transfer and sharing DoD's "lessons learned" from applicable exercises and program manage-

ment. **Such collaboration can increase the overall effectiveness of national capabilities and potentially reduce other agencies' dependencies on limited DoD assets.**

To succeed, the Department will need a systematic approach to ensure close coordination with the Department of Homeland Security and other interagency, state, and local partners, specifically:

- Facilitating the Department of Homeland Security's efforts to identify and provide appropriate defense technologies to state and local first responders;

- Nurturing new collaborative research, development, experimentation, test and acquisition opportunities with the Department of Homeland Security, while avoiding duplication of effort in these areas; and

- Ensuring the smooth transition of appropriate missions, technologies, and capabilities to the civil sector.

Complementing these activities will be a long-term effort with our Federal partners to identify specific, frequently requested DoD capabilities for possible transition to the civil sector.

Core Capability: Improved international partnership capacity and effective defense-to-defense relationships

Because it is the Department's first priority, homeland defense must be a central, carefully considered element of our defense relationships with key allies and friends abroad. The United States fosters strong defense relationships worldwide for many reasons of national security interest. Two such reasons are to strengthen allied military contributions to collective defense and to improve US capabilities through exposure to partners' expertise. Thus, DoD has an active security cooperation program that encourages mutual improvements to support coalition operations and to ensure interoperability. Clearly, our homeland defense will be substantially strengthened through the cooperation and assistance of allies. In turn, our allies can better protect their homelands if we help them build capacity for homeland defense and civil support. **We will strengthen DoD's emphasis in security cooperation on homeland defense and civil support, with particular focus on improved information sharing in defense-to-defense interactions.**

Our North American neighbors, Canada and Mexico, are vital to the protection of the US homeland and the continent. The Department also places special emphasis on cooperative homeland defense efforts with friendly nations in the Pacific and the Caribbean and with our NATO allies.

The primary mechanism for US-Canadian cooperation on homeland defense is the North American Aerospace Defense Command. Dedicated to the defense of US and Canadian airspace, NORAD has evolved from a Cold War institution to an agile 21st century counterterrorism capability reflecting an integrated, flexible bi-national approach to air defense. Over the next decade, the Department of Defense, in conjunction with the Department of State and the Department of Homeland Security, and working with our Canadian partners, will strengthen the NORAD concept by identifying mechanisms for sharing information across the air, maritime, and land operational domains— with shared awareness of the North American maritime domain as the first priority.

Given the importance of Mexico to US homeland defense, US-Mexican counter-terrorism cooperation is essential. The Department will work with the Department of Homeland Security, the Department of State, and Mexico to anticipate and plan for crisis coordination and consequence management following a terrorist attack. Cooperation with Mexico on law enforcement and immigration issues is substantial, especially in counternarcotics and border control operations. Defense cooperation requires similar emphasis and must be pursued with due respect for the Mexican government's policy goals and legal constraints. Traditional security assistance tools are pivotal in developing mutually beneficial defense capabilities and arrangements.

Just as defense of the US homeland begins well beyond our geographic boundaries, so too must our cooperative efforts to improve that defense. The expansion of information and intelligence sharing with foreign partners is critical to the success of this Strategy. Friendly and allied nations often possess significant information relating to terrorism, smuggling, and other US concerns.

Beyond the information realm, some nations have significant expertise to share with the United States in combating terrorism and other mission areas related to homeland defense. The United States likewise has much to gain in increasing the homeland defense capabilities of friendly nations. The Department will therefore expand combined education, exercise, training, and experimentation initiatives related to homeland defense.

V. Implications of the Strategy

"The threats and enemies we must confront have changed, and so must our forces."

The National Security Strategy of the United States of America

September 2002

The Strategy for Homeland Defense and Civil Support requires adjustments in DoD forces and capabilities, resource allocation, and technology development. Securing the US homeland is the first among many priorities outlined in the National Defense Strategy. Given resource constraints, this Strategy's objectives must be balanced against the Department's other requirements.

Force Structure

This Strategy reflects a Total Force approach to homeland defense missions, incorporating the capabilities of Active Duty, National Guard, and Reserve forces that will be trained and equipped primarily for warfighting missions in the forward regions and approaches. Forces must also be prepared to conduct the full spectrum of domestic civil support missions when directed by the President or the Secretary of Defense to do so.

To execute this diverse range of missions effectively, DoD must ensure the Total Force, both reserve and active components, is:

- *Timely* in response and readily accessible. Homeland defense and civil support missions require a rapid response, often measured in hours, not days.

- *Trained and equipped* to achieve the highest degree of readiness in a broad array of mission sets.

- *Transformed* to meet terrorist challenges. Timely, trained, and equipped forces must be agile and interoperable, taking advantage of networked capabilities.

Focused Reliance upon the Reserve Component

Homeland defense and civil support are Total Force responsibilities. However, the nation needs to focus particular attention on better using the competencies of National Guard and Reserve Component organizations. The National Guard is particularly well suited for civil support missions. As with other Reserve components, the National Guard is forward deployed in 3,200 communities through the nation. In addition, it is readily accessible in State Active Duty and Title 32 status, routinely exercised with local law enforcement, first responders, and the remainder of the Total Force, and experienced in supporting neighboring communities in times of crisis. In addition, Reserve forces currently provide many key homeland defense and civil support capabilities, including intelligence, military police, medical expertise, and chemical decontamination. The most promising areas for employment of the National Guard and Reserve forces are:

- *Air and Missile Defense,* including surveillance and manning of ground-based defense systems.

- *Maritime Security,* including Naval Reserve augmentation of active component and Coast Guard capabilities for intelligence and surveillance, critical infrastructure protection, port security, and maritime intercept operations. **The Naval Reserve should continue to transform to meet 21st century terrorist threats, with an emphasis on interdicting the maritime transport of CBRNE to the United States.**

- *Land defense*, including missions requiring Quick Reaction Forces/Rapid Reaction Forces. Reserve forces, including the National Guard, Army Reserve, and Marine Corps Reserve, are capable of serving in reaction force roles when sufficiently trained and resourced. For example, **the Army is considering whether to use existing National Guard force structure to form modular reaction forces, an initiative that could provide additional capabilities for domestic land defense.**

- *CBRNE response*, including capabilities for detection, extraction, decontamination, and medical care. Army Reserve chemical companies can provide significant capabilities for CBRNE assessment as well as extraction and decontamination of mass casualties. **The National Guard WMD Civil Support Teams, which will be located in all states and territories and the District of Columbia, can be federalized, if required. The National Guard Chemical-Biological-Radiological-High Explosives Enhanced Force Packages (NGCERFPs)** — task-organized from existing force structure — also could provide CBRNE response capabilities. The Reserve Component can also offer significant assistance with security, engineering, transportation, communications, medical response, and

many other CBRNE response needs. **The effective employment of National Guard forces in state, Title 32, or Title 10 status could increase the availability of other US military forces for overseas deployments.**

- *Critical Infrastructure Protection*, including the performance of comprehensive assessments of critical infrastructure sites and utilization of Reserve component forces for quick reaction requirements, when sufficiently trained and resourced, and local security at key defense and non-defense critical infrastructure sites, when directed.

Technology

Implementation of the Strategy for Homeland Defense and Civil Support may require several new technological investments. Three areas of particular interest for further exploration are advanced information and communications technology, new generations of sensors, and non-lethal capabilities.

Advanced Information and Communications Technology

Technological and organizational improvements for homeland security and homeland defense will benefit from focused investment in advanced information technology, especially to prevent, intercept, and respond to terrorist activity. Whether the objective is improved maritime domain awareness and operations, interception of weapons of mass destruction, response to chemical or biological attacks, or continuity of operations and government, improvement in information technology is critical to addressing current capability shortfalls. Advanced modeling and simulation techniques for threat identification, pattern analysis, risk assessment, dependency analysis, and cost/benefit calculus are critical for addressing issues of data sharing, security, and interoperability. Without these tools, the return on investments in other areas, such as improved sensors, detectors, command and control, and human intelligence collection and analysis, will be insufficient.

Equally pivotal are potential advances in communications technologies, particularly those supporting ground-mobile and airborne communications. DoD must reduce the size and power requirements of mobile communications systems and be able to shield them against electromagnetic effects.

Sensors

New generations of sensors and sensor platforms will improve threat awareness by helping to close current gaps over much of the maritime domain and in domestic air-space, particularly at low altitudes. Shared sensor technology could also play an important role in improving border surveillance by civilian agencies.

The placement of sensors on high altitude platforms, including new generations of unmanned aerial vehicles, satellites, and aerostats, could allow sustained surveillance of wide areas of the earth's surface. These sensors could also strengthen defenses against low-flying cruise missiles. Some new ground sensors are expected to have an over the horizon capability with applications for homeland defense and homeland security missions.

New sensor technologies could also have utility for: maritime defense, including the non-acoustic detection of underwater vehicles, objects, and swimmers; remote detection of concealed CBRNE weapons aboard ships; and mapping the location and extent of contamination should adversaries use these weapons. Finally, **DoD must fully integrate its sensors and others on which it relies with information networks to coordinate their use and rapidly distribute information.**

Non-Lethal Capabilities

As the terrorist attack of September 11, 2001, made it clear, we may be required to defeat attacks in major civilian population centers. Non-lethal capabilities hold some promise as an effective alternative to deadly force. The Department will therefore examine the potential operational employment of non-lethal weapons for homeland defense missions, particularly those where civilian loss of life can be effectively minimized.

Non-lethal technologies with potential application to homeland defense missions include:

- **Counter-personnel technology**, used to deny entry into a particular area, temporarily incapacitate individuals or groups, and clear facilities, structures, and areas.

- **Counter-material technology**, to disable, neutralize, or deny an area to vehicles, vessels, and aircraft, or disable particular items of equipment.

- **Counter-capability technology**, to disable or neutralize facilities, systems, and CBRNE.

The Department will expand basic research into the physiological effects of non-lethal weapons. The Department will also identify opportunities to share appropriate non-lethal capabilities with domestic law enforcement agencies, consistent with applicable law.

Rapid Prototyping of Emerging Capabilities

Advanced Concept Technology Demonstrations (ACTDs) are a key DoD vehicle for rapidly fielding promising technologies. The objectives of an ACTD are to conduct meaningful demonstrations of the capability, develop and test concepts of operations to optimize military effectiveness, and, if warranted, prepare to transition the capability into acquisition without loss of momentum. Currently, there are over 25 ACTDs with relevance to homeland defense and homeland security such as the Homeland Security/ Homeland Defense Command and Control Advanced Concept Technology Demonstration. The Department will ensure that requirements for homeland defense and civil support are properly addressed in the ACTD process. The Department will continue working with the Department of Homeland Security and other domestic and international partners to encourage their participation in ACTDs as appropriate. **DoD will also continue to leverage innovative capabilities arising from private sector initiatives, many of which are fostered through the interagency Technical Support Working Group (TSWG).**

Funding

Proper funding and budget oversight for homeland defense and CBRNE consequence management missions is vital. Currently, the Department accounts for homeland defense activities through a variety of disparate programs and funding lines in every Military Department and combatant command and numerous initiatives under the purview of the Office of the Secretary of Defense. Funding for homeland defense is not accounted for consistently.

Funding Implications

In developing planning and programming guidance to implement the Strategy for Homeland Defense and Civil Support, DoD must assess the fiscal implications of attaining and sustaining requisite core capabilities. Determining the relative costs and benefits of each of the following areas merit immediate attention:

- **Expanding communications infrastructure** and improving DoD's ability to share vital information while protecting the integrity of the Global Information Grid;

- **Improving intelligence assets** to improve overall threat awareness across all domains;

- Developing and procuring **advanced technologies** to maximize awareness of potential threats;

- Developing the capabilities needed to effectively conduct an active, layered **maritime defense** against transnational threats, including CBRNE attacks;

- Implementing DoD's **Defense Critical Infrastructure Protection** responsibilities;

- Furthering investments in the research, testing, and fielding of **non-lethal weapons** capabilities;

- Providing support for DoD **continuity of operations** in the event of a national emergency or catastrophe; and

- **Transforming the Reserve component** for homeland defense and civil support missions.

38

In the course of implementing this Strategy, the Department must not take on responsibilities and costs for homeland security missions better addressed by other Federal, state, local, or tribal authorities. This will require close cooperation with the Department of Homeland Security and other interagency partners.

Managing Homeland Defense and Civil Support Risks

The Department's risk management strategy acknowledges the importance of an active, layered homeland defense. **An active, layered defense integrates homeland defense and forward operations conceptually and operationally.** Therefore, the Department will assess homeland defense and civil support mission risks in the context of all of the requirements outlined in the National Defense Strategy.

The Strategy for Homeland Defense and Civil Support places a premium on the Department's primary responsibility for protecting the US homeland from attack. A second priority is to meet DoD's most challenging civil support mission—CBRNE consequence management. Specifically, the Strategy's risk management approach is as follows:

Lead. The Department's key lead objectives are to achieve maximum awareness of threats, deter, intercept, and defeat threats at a safe distance, and achieve mission assurance. **DoD must not accept undue risk in its active defense of the US homeland from direct air, land, or maritime threats.** The capability and readiness of US forces to intercept and defeat

these threats must be assured. Further, because the most critical element of successfully defeating threats to the US homeland is shared situational awareness, the Department will focus special attention in this area. DoD accepts some operational risk in achieving mission assurance.

Support. Transnational terrorists have a demonstrated intent to acquire weapons of mass destruction and exploit US vulnerabilities to employ such weapons against potential domestic targets. Accordingly, the Department will reduce risk by improving its consequence management capabilities for responding to multiple, simultaneous CBRNE mass casualty attacks in the United States. **DoD will maintain a ready, capable, and agile command and control structure, along with competently trained forces, to assist civilian authorities with catastrophic incident response. However, with the exception of a dedicated command and control element (currently the Joint Task Force-Civil Support) and the National Guard's WMD Civil Support Teams, DoD will continue to rely on dual-capable forces for consequence management and other defense support of civil authorities.** The Department minimizes the risk that dual-capable forces may be assigned to other high priority missions by deconflicting overseas and domestic force requirements wherever possible.

Enable. **The Department aims to decrease long-term risk by improving the capabilities of our interagency and international partners.** DoD accepts some risk in achieving the "Enable" objective to address other more immediate "Lead" and "Support" objectives.

VI. Conclusion

"The battle is now joined on many fronts. We will not waver; we will not tire; we will not falter; and we will not fail. Peace and freedom will prevail."

President George W. Bush
October 7, 2001

The United States faces ruthless enemies who seek to break our will by exploiting America's fundamental freedoms. Our adversaries are eager to employ violence against Americans at home. In this environment, the Department of Defense's paramount goal will continue to be the defense of the US homeland from direct attack.

A new kind of enemy requires a new concept for defending the US homeland. **The terrorist enemy now considers the US homeland a preeminent part of the global theater of combat, and so must we.** We cannot depend on passive or reactive defenses but must seize the initiative from adversaries.

The active, layered defense articulated in this Strategy seamlessly integrates US capabilities in the forward regions of the world, the global commons, the geographic approaches to the US territory, and within the United States. Whether in a leading, supporting, or enabling role, the Department of Defense, guided by this Strategy and consistent with US law, will work with an intense focus to protect the US homeland and the American people.

When fully realized, this Strategy will transform the Department's homeland defense and civil support capabilities. The nation will have effective intelligence, surveillance, and reconnaissance capabilities for homeland defense; and information will be widely shared with relevant decision-makers. The Department will execute homeland defense missions with well-trained and responsive forces that use improved technology and operational concepts to eliminate seams between the maritime, air, and land domains. Additionally, **the Department will achieve unity of effort with our interagency and international partners in executing homeland defense and civil support missions.**

The effectiveness of any strategy is ultimately in the hands of those charged with its implementation. The Department of Defense will carefully consider the potential implications of this Strategy for force structure, technology, and funding. It will also continually reevaluate the Strategy, adapting it as needed for the dynamic international environment and changing US policy and capabilities.

The Department of Defense must change its conceptual approach to homeland defense. The Department can no longer think in terms of the "home" game and the "away" game. There is only one game. The Strategy for Homeland Defense and Civil Support is a significant step toward this strategic transformation. Defending the US homeland—our people, property, and freedom—is our most fundamental duty. Failure is not an option.

www.ingramcontent.com/pod-product-compliance
Lightning Source LLC
Chambersburg PA
CBHW080623290526
45790CB00007B/2904